ENCOURAGING MOMENTS

——— WITH ———

BOBBY WILLIAMS ®

> **"52 Weeks of Inspiration for Your Daily Walk with Christ"**

Bobby@A3Marketing.com
Hendersonville, Tennessee
May 2021

ISBN: 978-0-9795061-1-6 Paperback
ISBN: 978-0-9795061-2-3 E-Book

This book contains scripture from the King James Version of the Bible,
which is in the public domain.

Front cover image by Adrian David Payne Photography
Book design by Chris Cunningham
Editor- Sharon Felton

Printed by Ingram Book Group., in the United States of America

First printing edition: May 2021

Spirit of a Champion Inc. Publishing
170 E Main Street #118
Hendersonville, TN 37075
615-207-4396

EncouragingMoments.com

FOREWORD

It is a rare and precious moment in life when God allows you to meet someone who looks like Jesus. I had that privilege when I met Bobby Williams. Over time the fellowship he and I have enjoyed has only increased my respect for the gift of God in him.

As you read this book it will become apparent that encouragement is the ministry that the Father has entrusted to Bobby.

In the uncertain moments that we all live in, encouragement to stand strong and believe that God holds us in His arms is needed.

The words you are about to read don't come from a vessel that has not been broken, but from a child of God who walked through the valley of the shadow of death and emerged on the other side with the shout of victory. May this book take you on a journey that at the end the shout of triumph will be in your heart!

- Kent Christmas
Pastor of Regeneration Nashville

PREFACE

This weekly devotion book was written for those striving to maximize each day in the Lord. I seek to help my readers to become the best they could be, to be inspired through Christian inspiration, and to be empowered and encouraged to live the victorious life Jesus promised in John 10:10.

When I first heard God's calling me at my home church to start producing a 1-minute Biblical message for TV to encourage others, I would have never imagined the impact these small moments would have in Tennessee, across the nation, and in my personal life. I am so thankful to God for the many thank you notes, texts, emails, phone calls, and personal testimonies from others of how *Encouraging Moments with Bobby Williams* has helped them with their walk with God. From the very beginning, they were created out of obedience to the Lord, to glorify His name, and to build up His church.

God used all of my family and friends to rally around me for this cause. My wife Donna, our son Robert, and daughter Tori all believed in me and the calling God had placed on my life; they could see that *Encouraging Moments with Bobby Williams* was another step in the journey. I have had the privilege to be entrusted by God with the message of encouragement, whether in the marketplace, in church, or in the media and I thank Him publicly for this great honor.

52 *Encouraging Moments* was written for those Christians who like me, as a young Christian was striving for a deeper walk in the Lord, but didn't understand all that God had for me, nor how to get there. I so wanted the abundant, victorious life that Jesus had promised. I wanted more peace in my life and less worry. I wanted more trust, and less doubt. I wanted His will and His direction, so I completely surrendered my life to God, and the results have been amazing. I have found the Victorious life and want to share it with you!

After 35 years of Bible study through the empowerment of Holy Spirit and my years of experience as a teacher, deacon, and inspirational minister, I have chosen these 52 God-inspiring moments, one for each week of the year, plus two bonus weeks that are sure to impact your life in a positive manner. They are the best of the best short devotions for those who are still learning, still wanting a closer relationship with Jesus and have a burning desire to be inspired each day.

My prayer is that each one will deepen your Faith, increase your Self-confidence, give you more Peace, more Love, more Joy, more Courage, and more Hope for a better tomorrow. As a Christian, there is a better way to live, and that life is a life based on a strong relationship with Jesus Christ as your personal Savior. You were born to win!

Love you in the Lord!
BW

This Book is dedicated to my lovely virtuous wife Donna V. Williams for 35 years of marriage. She has been my greatest gift from God. I love her with all my heart for loving me unconditionally and always supporting me in all my dreams!

Love you!
Bobby

1

FROM FEAR TO FAITH

My prayer today is that someone who is fearful would walk away from this encouraging moment with more courage, more hope for the future, and a deeper trust in God. I pray that any fears that are holding you back from the abundant life God has for you would be washed away, through the hearing of His word and this message.

What fearful things are you facing today? Illness, financial crisis, loss of a loved one, loss of job, a troubled relationship, a wayward child, an addiction problem, anxiety, fear of the future, fear of loss, fear of a bad economy, fear of death, fear of failure?

Fear is: **F**alse **E**vidence **A**ppearing **R**eal.

Most all our fears never come to pass, but when we **focus** on fear it can take control over our lives in such a way that we are paralyzed from moving forward with God's plan of Success for us. Faith can take a backseat to fear, and it can be devastating, even to the believer. Believe me, I understand Fear: it can cause anxiety attacks, bad decisions, and cause us to miss God's best for our lives. But I have great news for you today. God wants to lead you out of Fear and into Faith. Let's examine the word FAITH: **F**orsaking **A**ll **I**'ll T**RUST** **H**IM. Instead of relying on yourself, look up to the heavens and to God for answers. It's not in His plan for you to live a fearful life.

2nd Timothy 1:7 says, [7] For God hath not given us the spirit of fear; but of power, and of love, and of a sound mind.

See God's plan for you, is not to fear. His plan promises we can be confident in God, courageous, strong, and enjoy a faith-driven, exciting life, in which we can TRUST him through FAITH and fear not. Our focus needs to be fixed on God and not on our fears.

Say these words over and over today: FAITH is: Forsaking ALL I'll TRUST HIM. Today walk from Fear to FAITH and into Trust for everything!

2

TAKE COURAGE

Take Courage, God is with you! No matter how badly your circumstances are today. No matter what adversity you are facing. No matter what trial you may be experiencing! Know that God's divine power will be with you through the test, through the discouragement, through the loss, and through what you feel is an uncertain future. Take Courage, for God is with you!

The Bible says: He will never leave you nor forsake you!

If you have accepted Jesus Christ as your personal Savior, then you can count on God to show up and help you in your time of need! He will never leave you nor forsake you as the Bible promises in Deuteronomy 31. In this chapter of the Old Testament, Moses was 120 years old and he was turning over his leadership to Joshua. He had all of Israel together and gave them the below promise.

Deuteronomy 31:1,6 And Moses went and spake these words unto all Israel.

6 Be strong and of a good courage, fear not, nor be afraid of them: for the Lord thy God, he it is that doth go with thee; he will not fail thee, nor forsake thee.

7 And Moses called unto Joshua, and said unto him in the sight of all Israel, Be strong and of a good courage: for thou must go with this people unto the land which the Lord hath sworn unto their fathers to give them; and thou shalt cause them to inherit it.

8 And the Lord, he it is that doth go before thee; he will be with thee, he will not fail thee, neither forsake thee: fear not, neither be dismayed.

God is walking with you through the trial you are facing today! Be sure to take the burden you are facing to God in prayer and believe the above scripture. You can take courage, because the one who created you will see your through! He will make a way for you! Keep praying! Keep believing! Be strong and courageous! You are a child of the most-high living GOD! He will never leave you or forsake you!

3

UNDERSTANDING THE POWER OF THE HOLY SPIRIT!

God lives inside every believer, empowering them each day to become more like Christ and live the victorious life Jesus wanted for His followers. Upon accepting Jesus Christ as your Lord and Savior, every believer receives the seal of the Holy Spirit.

Ephesians 1:13 And you also were included in Christ when you heard the message of truth, the gospel of your salvation. When you believed, you were marked in Him with a SEAL, the promised Holy Spirit. Christ lives in us through His Holy Spirit. His Seal on all Christians. Since Jesus Christ is no longer on earth in the flesh, He sent the Holy Spirit to EMPOWER US through every chapter of our lives. Jesus said in Luke 24:49 I am going to send you what my Father has promised; but stay in the city until you have been clothed with POWER from on high.

That Power is the Holy Spirit! God in us!

In John 14:16 Jesus says: And I will ask the Father, and He will give you another advocate to help you and be with you forever, the Spirit of Truth. 17. The world cannot accept him, because it neither sees him nor knows him. But you know Him, for He lives with you and will be in you.

Ignite the power of the Holy Spirit living inside of you through Prayer, Bible study, listening to God, asking for His wisdom, His favor, His forgiveness, and His will for you each day. Seek the Lord every morning, thanking Him and praising His Holy name! The Holy Spirit will EMPOWER you to do great things for the Lord and have the victory in this life you so desire! The Holy Spirit lives in us to EMPOWER our Christian walk with God! Praise His Holy name! Walk in the Spirit! Sing in the Spirit! Pray in the Spirit and have Victory in the Spirit!

4

WITH   GOD   ALL   THINGS   ARE   POSSIBLE

Too many people today do not understand who God truly is. They question His Authority, His Ability, and His Sovereignty in our lives. He is the Creator of the Universe, and nothing was created in the Universe without Him! Nature itself answers to Him. Nothing is impossible for our great and wonderful living God! In the natural your situation might look hopeless! In the natural it might look impossible! In the natural, is easy to get down and feel like your prayers won't be answered! But with God all things are possible!

Remember the character of God will not allow Him to fail us!

God is Omnipresent – always present with us!

God is Omniscient – meaning He is all knowing!

God is Omnipotent – Unlimited power!

Remember Jesus' words in Mark 10:27: Jesus said with men it is impossible, but not with God: for with God all things are possible.

So, whatever you are facing today, that seems impossible to fix, take it to God and what seems impossible to man, will be possible through God. The supernatural power of God will help you!

With GOD ALL THINGS ARE POSSIBLE!

5

BE STRONG IN THE LORD! PLACE YOUR HOPE IN GOD!

Everyone can feel weak physically and mentally at times in their lives. Sometimes we feel exhausted and wonder how we will make it through our current workload and family responsibilities we have in our lives. Stress from family issues, work issues, and relationships can be so hard at times. In saying all of that I remember the scripture I can do all things through Christ who strengthens me! Philippians 4:13.

You see, God is the source of all our strength! God promises in Isaiah 40:29-31 to renew our strength as we place our HOPE in HIM!

It says: He gives strength to the weary and increases the power of the weak!

30. Even youths grow tired and weary and young men stumble and fall; 31 but those who Hope in the Lord will renew their strength. They will soar on wings like eagles;

they will run and not grow weary, they will walk and not faint.

Place all HOPE in Jesus Christ! Remember HE gives strength to the weary and increases the power of the weak! Whenever I feel discouraged, down, or weak, I go before the Lord in prayer. Once before the Lord, I will say Lord you have promised in Isaiah 40 to give strength to the weary and increase the power of the weak! Please help me Father at this time of need! Give me your Strength and power to overcome this situation in my life as I place all HOPE in you. In Jesus' name! After that prayer I feel renewed! My hope increases! God's power in my life allows me to regain my strength and carry onward! Go before Him today! He will renew your strength and you will fly again like a soaring eagle! You will run and not grow weary! You will walk and not faint! God is with you!

6

GAINING A STRONGER SELF-CONFIDENCE!

If you are struggling with a low self-confidence issue about yourself, you may not realize how much God really loves and values your life. What a great future and a hope He has for you. How beautiful, unique, and special you truly are. You may not understand that you were made in the image of God! That's what I said.

The Bible in the book of Genesis 1:27 says:

So, God created mankind in His own image, in the image of God He created them; male and female He created them.

Low self-esteem issues can be derived by what a person thinks about themselves. These false and negative thoughts can make you feel unworthy, and less than you should. Sometimes people feel like they're not beautiful or handsome enough, not the right shape, not the right size, feel too thin, too fat, too bald, not athletic enough, and more. Low self-esteem issues can be brought about by negative things people have said about us. Other low self- esteem thoughts come from past failures, sin, and bad decisions in our lives. Whatever the low self-confidence issue is, God doesn't want you to live without a strong self-confidence. His plan for a strong self-confidence is found only through a personal relationship with Jesus Christ, where our value is based upon what God says about us and not what we think or feel.

God has made you unique in this world. No one has your fingerprints, no one has your exact features. No one has your destiny! If you are a born-again Christian, then turn over every low self-esteem thought you have to the Lord! Ask Him to give you a stronger self-confidence based on what He has said in His Word about you! This week, read the below scriptures to gain a stronger self-confidence! Embrace who you are in the Lord! How wonderful, how special, how beautiful, and how loved you are by God!

Psalms 139:14: I praise you because I am fearfully and wonderfully made.
Psalms 28:7: The Lord is my strength and my shield; my heart trusts in Him, and He helps me. My heart leaps for Joy, and with my song I praise him.

7

DON'T WORRY!

Don't worry! Don't worry! Let it go! Bring all of your worries and burdens to God. Place your trust in God, and not in yourself! As you trust him, He will work things out for you! Worrying about your situation, losing sleep, having anxiety attacks, or being fearful about today and tomorrow won't change a thing! 97% of everything we worry about, never happens! So, glance at the problem, but focus all your thoughts on the Lord Jesus Christ, the one who can give you the peace you need as He leads you to victory through the current trial or crisis you find yourself in. You may be worrying right now as I am speaking these encouraging words to you today! God didn't create you to worry your life away!

In Philippians 4:6-7 it says:
⁶ Do not be anxious about anything, but in everything by prayer and supplication with thanksgiving let your requests be made known to God. ⁷ And the peace of God, which surpasses all understanding, will guard your hearts and your minds in Christ Jesus.

God is able to fix your situation. You must be willing to go to him with a thankful, humble, heart, and let him know what you need Him to help you with. Whatever the need, He will answer your prayer. He promises that His peace will guard your heart and mind. God will take away all fear, all worries, all doubts as you continue to bring your needs before him and trust Him. Even in a great storm or trial in your life God promises His peace!

Jesus said in Matthew 6:34: So do not worry about tomorrow; for tomorrow will care for itself. Each day has enough trouble of its own.

Worrying won't change anything, so on this day, this glorious day in the Lord! Be encouraged! Place all of your trust in Jesus Christ and He will work it out for you! Trust God! He loves you and He will make a way for you! So do not worry, God will see you through!

8

DON'T GIVE UP ON YOUR DREAMS!

BELIEVE!

You may be thinking about quitting. About giving up! About calling it quits! Don't give up on your dreams! It's a new year! Believe again! It's not time to quit, it's time to get on the offense! It's time to think positive thoughts! It's time to believe again! It's time to dream again!

God has great plans for you and your life!

In Jeremiah 29:11 God says:

For I know the plans I have for YOU, declares the Lord, plans to prosper YOU, and not to harm YOU, plans to GIVE YOU a HOPE and a FUTURE.

Trust the above scripture to understand that God has great plans that include prospering you! Plans to help you fulfill

your dreams! To give you a hope and a future. As you continue to believe and take your dreams, hopes, and plans to God HE WILL BLESS YOU! Keep reading the scripture of Jeremiah 29:11 over and over and over again this week and accept God's promise for your life!

Memorize this scripture on your heart and Believe! God loves you and will help! Step out in Faith!

Ephesians 3:20 says: God will immensely bless you more than you can ask or think!

So with God behind you, backing your every move! Don't give up on your dreams for He is the dream maker! He will help you fulfill your God given destiny!

9

GOD'S WISDOM IS SUPREME

No one can give you advice like God himself. Search the scriptures in the Bible about God's Wisdom because it is the Wisdom of God. Consult with God before making a big purchase, before making a move, before changing a career, before quitting a job, before marrying someone, before dissolving a relationship, what to do in uncertain times, and more. Take all of your plans to Him and let Him help you make all of these decisions. Ask Him for His Wisdom in every situation.

In Proverbs chapter 4:7 it says that God's wisdom is supreme. So acquire wisdom. And whatever you may acquire, gain understanding. God is saying Get wisdom, get understanding, do not forget my words or swerve from them. Don't look to the world for answers. Go to God's word. Place his wisdom in your heart. It will protect your life, add years to your life. God's wisdom will be the source of a blessed life!

Proverbs 3:5-6

5 Trust in the LORD with all your heart, And lean not on your own understanding;

6 In all your ways acknowledge Him, and He will make your paths straight.

As you live your life day by day focus on all the scriptures of Wisdom in the Bible. Make all of your decisions by asking for Gods direction, God's Wisdom. If you feel inadequate or want more wisdom, James 1:5 says: Now if any of you lacks wisdom, he or she should ask God, who gives generously to all without finding fault, and it will be given to him.

So, go to God to receive His Wisdom, His direction and His understanding that only He can give! Pray over every decision and wait for the Lord to direct your steps. He promises us He will do this for us. Remember God's Wisdom is Supreme!

10

BELIEVE   GOD   –   FAITH   THAT   WINS!

Many people today are believing in idols that replace God's power, His authority, His sovereignty, and His direction for their lives. They live a defeated lifestyle without hope for a future depending on themselves, on friends, on events, career, degree, or something else in life to make them happy. Like a lost ship at sea without a rudder, they are tossed by every wind, wave, and storm that hits their lives. Searching for life's answers, but always becoming a victim without God's direction. Christians who totally believe God have Faith that wins. Instead of being a victim, believers can be victors no matter what happens to them in life. I have three major points to help you achieve a Faith that wins.

#1. Believe God for everything!

Romans 10:9 says if you declare with your mouth Jesus is Lord and believe with your heart that God raised Him from the dead, you will be saved.

#2. Dedicate your LIFE to God

Matt 22:37: Jesus said, Love the Lord your God with all your heart and with all your soul and with all your mind.

#3. Trust Everything to God: all future plans, hopes, and dreams!

Hebrews 11:1: Now Faith is the confidence in what we hope for and the assurance of what we do not see.

This week come back to these scriptures and ask God to give you complete understanding. Do you Believe God for everything in your life? Have you been living a fully dedicated life to the Lord? Do you love Him more than the world? Do you trust Him with everything in your life? Only you know the answer to these questions, but I encourage you to BELIEVE GOD and YOU WILL HAVE A FAITH THAT WINS!

11

GOD IS THE GOD OF RESTORATION

You may feel like a failure. You may be upset with yourself over past decisions and past failures. Maybe you made a bad decision in a relationship, a costly financial decision, or got into a fight with someone you love. Maybe you lost your temper, maybe you have been drinking too much, doing drugs, or lying to someone. Maybe you haven't kept your promises to others, stopped going to church, or not reading your Bible. Maybe worse.

Whatever the case may be, we have all sinned and missed the mark. The Bible says in Romans 3:23: "For all have sinned, and come short of the glory of God." Sin brings on a guilty conscious, a broken lifestyle, and great sadness in one's life. Just know, it's not too late! We serve an all-powerful, forgiving God, who sent His only Son to die on a cross, to shed His blood for all our sins, and to be raised from the dead on the third day. Jesus died for our sins. The shedding of His blood covered our sin, so that God would allow us a place in Heaven. So that we would be made Holy and acceptable in God's eyes. The Bible says that His blood makes us whiter than snow.

Isaiah 1:18: "Though your sins be as scarlet, they shall be whiter than snow."

If you're already a Christian and need forgiveness, just ask God using the scripture 1st John 1:9 below in your prayer and He will forgive and restore you, as you turn away from that sin or bad lifestyle you have been living. Be specific about what you did and ask for Him to not only forgive you, but to keep you from sinning again. As you bring this before the Lord, HE WILL FORGIVE YOU!

Once forgiven, forgive yourself, and move forward. If you have offended anyone, try and make amends. Leave the burden of guilt at Jesus Christ's feet in prayer. God is the GOD OF RESTORATION! He will restore you! If you are serious about wanting to walk in the light of Christ, stay away from sin in your life. Be sure to walk Holy unto God each day by following Him and being obedient to His commandments.

1st John 1:9: If we confess our sins, he is faithful and just to forgive us our sins and purify us from all unrighteousness.

12

FACING THE GIANTS IN YOUR LIFE!

I want to talk to you today about facing the Giants in your life. Those fearful things that keep holding you back. What trial are you facing? Are you trying to fight your Giant alone or are you asking God for help? Fear can keep you from God's best!

Whatever Giant you are facing, whether a financial crisis, a health issue, a loss you've experienced, or an unanswered prayer. I am here to tell you that God will help you conquer that giant in your life! King David, as a young boy was literally faced with a Giant named Goliath from the Philistine Army! Goliath was about 10 feet tall and David as a young man was around 5 feet tall. Goliath was a proven warrior with giant armor and very strong. Each day, Goliath would come out and taught the army of Israel, but none of the men were brave enough to fight Goliath. So many people around David told him there was no way he could fight this giant and win. They said he was too young, too weak, too small. But David had God with him, and God gave him great courage to fight the giant in his life.

1 Samuel 17:
[37] David said moreover, The Lord that delivered me out of the paw of the lion, and out of the paw of the bear, he will deliver me out of the hand of this Philistine. And Saul said unto David, Go, and the Lord be with thee.
[45] Then said David to the Philistine, Thou comest to me with a sword, and with a spear, and with a shield: but I come to thee in the name of the Lord of hosts, the God of the armies of Israel, whom thou hast defied.
[46] This day will the Lord deliver thee into mine hand;

And David, with God's help and one round stone, killed the Giant in his life. He won the Victory! Take the Giant you are fearing in your life to God and He will help you to conquer that Giant. Just like King David, you will win! You will have the victory over the Giant in your life! Victory will be yours! Take it to God in prayer! He will fight this battle for you! Even if the odds are against you!

13

THE *POWER* OF *PRAYER*

James 5:16: "The effectual fervent prayer of a righteous man availeth much."

Nothing has impacted my life more than answered prayer. God wants an intimate relationship with you, and going to Him in prayer grows that relationship. Prayer should be the top priority of every Christian. The Bible says to pray about everything. Take all things to God in prayer!

In Matthew 7:7-8 the Bible says, "Ask and it shall be given to you: seek and you shall find, knock and the door will be opened to you." [8] For everyone who asks receives. To have a successful life in Christ, we need to always pray to him about everything. With God as your partner, he will answer your prayers!

Here is a prescription on how to pray.

#1. Get alone with God and pray 10 to 20 minutes a day.
I like my prayer closet at home because it is dark and quiet. Others like to pray in a boat, in the forest, in a bonus room, in the backyard, or in their car. Just pick a place where you can be alone with God without distractions and pray at least 20 minutes a day. In Matthew chapter 26, Jesus prays alone to the Father in the garden of Gethsemane. He also prayed throughout His ministry alone in many other chapters in the Bible. Remember Jesus gave us His example on how to get alone and pray. So, trust His lead on praying alone in a quiet place. It will change your life.

#2. Always have a Bible promises book or Bible verse in your prayer that has to do with the prayer you are asking God to answer. For i nce, I might use Ephesians 3:20 that says, God will do more than we can ask or think. For any subject you are praying about, there is a verse to go along with your prayer. **Prayer + God's word = Success**

#3. Write your prayers down in a prayer journal. Date them and then look back over the months and years, to see how God answered your prayers! This will build your FAITH and TRUST in knowing that GOD HIMSELF is answering your prayers and cares about even the smallest details in your life. Philippians 4:6: Do not be anxious about anything, but in every situation by prayer and petition, with thanksgiving, present your requests to God.

14

AGREEMENT PRAYER! THE POWER OF 2 OR MORE IN PRAYER

A one cord rope is strong, but a two-cord rope is twice as strong as the one cord rope. In the Bible, Jesus has a teaching about prayer in Matthew 18. I call this the "agreement prayer" and it is very, very powerful.

Matthew 18: 19-20: "Again, truly I tell you, that if two of you on earth agree about anything they ask for, it will be done for them by my Father in Heaven. [20] For where two or three gather in my name, there am I with them."

This powerful lesson on **prayer** is a **special key** that will help **your prayers be answered.** If you are a man choose another Godly man as your prayer partner. If you are a woman then choose another Godly woman to pray with you in this way. Make sure you can trust them for complete confidence. Not sharing what you discuss or pray about with others. Write down some specific things together that you are praying for. Things that each person needs prayer about.

An example of a prayer that was answered for myself and my prayer partner was that a little girl in my prayer partner's church had been under water in a pool and was in a coma at the hospital. Of course, everyone wanted her to come out of the coma, but also not to have brain damage, since she was under water several minutes and had been life flighted to another city for treatment because she lived in a small town without a major hospital. Even now I get teared up since this little 4-year-old girl woke up the next day from answered prayer, and her first words were "I want some pizza!" She was alive and had no brain damage. God answered our prayer that night! We praised His Holy name! We cried about His love and mercy! He will answer your prayers as well. I realize not every prayer will be so miraculous, but what I do know is that this type of prayer is **very powerful** and as you practice praying with another person, you will see the hand of God move and answer your prayers. Pray for all the prayers each one of you brings to the other. Use Matthew 18:19-20 as your scripture, your Bible Promise from God and watch Him answer your prayers.

15

JESUS WILL CALM THE STORM IN YOUR LIFE!

No matter what storm your facing in life, God will see you through! You may be faced with a financial hardship, a broken relationship, the loss of a loved one, or worse, but know that our great God will calm the storm and bring peace back into your life. It's our job not to focus on the winds and the waves! No, we must focus on the Lord himself! Focus on the one who can get you through this storm and to safety.

In Mark 4:35-41 Jesus calms the storm and saves the disciples from drowning!

³⁵ And the same day, when the even was come, he saith unto them, Let us pass over unto the other side.

³⁶ And when they had sent away the multitude, they took him even as he was in the ship. And there were also with him other little ships.

³⁷ And there arose a great storm of wind, and the waves beat into the ship, so that it was now full.

³⁸ And he was in the hinder part of the ship, asleep on a pillow: and they awake him, and say unto him, Master, carest thou not that we perish?

³⁹ And he arose, and rebuked the wind, and said unto the sea, Peace, be still. And the wind ceased, and there was a great calm.

⁴⁰ And he said unto them, Why are ye so fearful? how is it that ye have no faith?

⁴¹ And they feared exceedingly, and said one to another, What manner of man is this, that even the wind and the sea obey him? Just like He calmed the storm for the disciples, He will do it for you! Start praising God for the victory over the storm in your life! Focus on Jesus Christ and the things of the Lord! Don't look at the winds and the waves! You have His favor! Blessings are coming your way as you trust Him! Victory in Jesus!

16

READ YOUR BIBLE DAILY FOR INSPIRATION

The Bible is the inspired infallible word of GOD. It is absolute truth! It will inspire you each day of your life and instruct you on the way to go as you read the Word! It will uplift your spirit daily and grow your Faith in Jesus Christ! It will open up possibilities, change fear to Faith, doubt into trust, and bring you a hope for a great future! Read it daily!

In 2 Timothy 3:16-17 the Bible says that:
[16] All scripture is given by inspiration of God, and is profitable for doctrine, for reproof, for correction, for instruction in righteousness:
[17] That the man of God may be perfect, thoroughly furnished unto all good works.

Scripture is used to inspire us, to teach us the doctrine of the Bible, its principles, it' commandments, knowledge, wisdom, for correction in our lives and for instruction in righteousness. To protect us, and more!

Proverbs 2:6: For the Lord gives wisdom; from His mouth come knowledge and understanding.

The Bible is God's great love letter to His people! Read it and be blessed! Every day I read my Bible before leaving the house for work. Each day God teaches me what I need for that day and my Word for the week from Him.

I gain such understanding, peace through any storm, and trust His Word over all others! The Word of God is so amazing! It has helped me through the best and the worst times of my life! It has changed my thinking, my attitude and has helped me to become more like Christ. Blessings to you as you read the Word of God each day!

Psalms 119:105: Your word is a lamp for my feet, a light on my path.

Armor of God

Eph 6:14-17

17

PUT ON THE FULL ARMOR OF GOD FOR PROTECTION

Our battle in this world is a Spiritual battle! It requires taking on the full armor of God. The powers of the dark world, the devil's schemes are everywhere, trying to victimize and destroy the lives of people. Hoping to ruin their lives and steal their soul. But thanks be to God, that we can be victors and not victims in this life, if we take on the full armor of God. To be in Christ is to be a dedicated follower. To be dedicated to His Word. To walk with Him. To talk with Him. To Pray to Him. To Love Him.

Ephesians 6:11-17 in the Bible explains what the Christian should do to be able to stand against the devil's schemes.
[11] Put on the whole armor of God, that ye may be able to stand against the wiles of the devil.
[12] For we wrestle not against flesh and blood, but against principalities, against powers, against the rulers of the darkness of this world, against spiritual wickedness in high places.
[13] Wherefore take unto you the whole armor of God, that ye may be able to withstand in the evil day, and having done all, to stand.
[14] Stand therefore, having your loins girt about with truth, and having on the breastplate of righteousness;
[15] And your feet shod with the preparation of the gospel of peace;
[16] Above all, taking the shield of faith, wherewith ye shall be able to quench all the fiery darts of the wicked.
[17] And take the helmet of salvation, and the sword of the Spirit, which is the word of God

If you're born again, you have the helmet of Salvation, a guaranteed place in Heaven with Jesus. The breastplate of Righteousness is being like Christ; honest, good, humble, and fair to others. Having His righteousness shine through our lives. The Belt of Truth is the truth of what the Bible says over what the world tells us to believe. The Sword of the Spirit is the Word of God, an offensive weapon because when we share with others the Good News of Jesus Christ, the Holy Spirit, leads them to see their sins and to want to be forgiven. All of this Armor leads to the Favor of God in our lives and protects us from the world and the schemes of the devil. Be encouraged! God's armor never fails us!

18

PRAISING GOD IN PRAYER

Praising God in your prayers shows Him how much you love Him and acknowledges His greatness. Praising God shows appreciation to Him for all He is. He is the Creator of the Universe! He is the great I am! He is the Alpha and Omega! The First and the Last! He is the one and true living God! He spoke the world into existence with just His word! Praise His Holy name!

Praising God in your prayers will bring the Joy of the Lord to you during your prayer. Look up to the Heavens and Praise Him for His greatness! The presence of the Holy Spirit will be upon you and fill you with His great joy as you praise His Holy name!

In prayer, always praise His name and Joy will fill your heart, even if you are having a tough day.

Here is a scripture about praising God!

Psalms 33:2-3: Praise the Lord with Harp: sing unto him with the psaltery and an instrument of ten strings. Sing unto Him a new song; play skillfully with a loud noise.

Praise the Lord and see His mighty power in your life! God loves you and wants a personal relationship with you. We have an awesome God. If we Acknowledge Him and humble ourselves before Him; He is pleased and fills our hearts with His unspeakable JOY! Praise the Lord!

19

THANKSGIVING PRAYER

Every day when I go outside, I look up into the sky and thank God for all the many blessings in my life. I know He can hear and see me, so I never forget to Thank Him! Thanking Him for all the good things God has done, for all the blessings.

The Bible says in James 1:17: "Every good gift and every perfect gift is from above and cometh down from the Father of lights with whom is no variableness, neither shadow of turning."

Where does one begin to thank God for all He has done? Regularly I first thank Him for sending His Son Jesus Christ and for saving a sinner like me. I thank Him for my wife, our children, family, and friends. I thank Him for our health, church, and country. I thank Him for the Holy Spirit, for our relationship and the love He has for us. I thank Him for my being written into the Book of Life.

Psalms 95:2 says, "Let us come before His presence with thanksgiving, and make a joyful noise unto Him with psalms."

Psalms 100:4 says, "Enter His gates with Thanksgiving, and into His courts with praise: be thankful unto Him and bless His name."

We are to come to God in prayer with a thankful heart. Take a survey of all the many things God has done for you. Take time out every day to Thank God for all of your blessings.

Hebrews 13:15-16 tells every Christian what they should do by saying, "By Him therefore, let us offer the sacrifice of praise to God continually, that is, the fruit of our lips giving thanks to His name. But to do good and to communicate forget not: for with such sacrifices God is well pleased."

Don't focus on what you don't have; count your many blessings! A thankful heart shows God that YOU appreciate the gifts He has given you. GOD is so GREAT and is so GOOD TO ALL of US! Thank God every day for all of your blessings! He will hear you and be pleased with you!

20

PRAYER OF CONFESSION

The apostle John wrote in 1 John 1:9-10: "If we confess our sins, he is faithful and just to forgive us our sins, and to cleanse us from all unrighteousness. If we say that we have not sinned we make him a liar, and his word is not in us." 1 Peter 1:16: "for it is written, Be ye Holy; for I am holy."

The Bible tells us that we have all fallen short of the Glory of God. Each day we should ask for the forgiveness of our sins. Sin separates us, it distances us from God, and harms our relationships with others. He requires us to follow His commandments to be Holy unto God. Sometimes we don't even realize that we have missed the mark, so I make sure I have confessed my sin every day, so that I can be forgiven for even ones that I don't realize I have committed. I am not suggesting that Christ's Salvation will ever expire; rather, as we grow as Christians we will still have some thoughts, words, and actions that unless confessed can keep God from answering our prayers. Quite simply, we will sin sometimes since we are human and still in this world. But through the shedding of Christ's blood on the cross we are no longer a slave to sin.

Every day in my own life I have to take an inventory of how I have acted, what I have said, and if there is any sin that I need to confess. I want my life to be more Christ-like each day! I want his plan for my life and that includes being Holy unto God through the power of His Holy Spirit and His Word. I surrender each day to what he wants for I am an ambassador of Jesus Christ and want to be more like Him.

Isaiah 59:2 says your sins have hid His face from you that He will not hear.

Confessing your sins to God brings you back under his authority and enables your prayers to be more easily answered. We all want God's best for our lives and that entails that we would not sin against Him and if we do, even in a small way, we quickly fall on our knees in prayer and ask forgiveness and turn away from it, so that our Father in heaven would be pleased with us and answer our prayers. Thank you, God for sending your Son for the forgiveness of sins. Thank you for your great mercy! Thank you for washing us whiter than snow!

21

PETITION PRAYER: ASK AND IT SHALL BE GIVEN

In your prayer life you should be asking God for your needs and deepest desires. Really it is asking Him for every need, as children would go to their father and mother.

Philippians 4:6 says, "Be careful for nothing; but in everything by prayer and supplication with thanksgiving let your requests be made known unto God." Bring your worries, troubles, trials, sickness, sins, needs, desires, all of your hopes to God.

Psalms 37:4 says the "Delight thyself also in the Lord, and He shall give thee the desires of Thine Heart!"

God rewards those who are faithful, those who put their full trust in Him and not other things. God cares about every detail in your life and wants to be part of all your hopes and dreams. Go to God for your every need – everything!

Remember, we do the asking and God decides what is best for us! God's answers are always best for his children. Many people don't receive what they desire in life simply for not asking God for their desires.

Matthew 7:7 tells us simply "Ask and it shall be given you; seek, and you shall find; knock, and it shall be opened unto you.

God wants a personal relationship with you in every area of your life. As you partner with him in prayer, He himself will fulfill the deepest desires of your heart and take you places you never thought were possible. Don't go it alone: ask God in Faith, to help you! Keep the Faith and watch God answer your prayers! He loves you and wants to bless you!

22

LISTENING TO GOD

Listening to God is such a powerful thing in a Christian's life and yet I struggled with this for many years. Finally, the troubles, trials, and worries of my life drove me into a deep prayer life. I am so thankful for those tough moments that grew my Faith and my relationship with God. My breakthrough came from studying the Bible and being devoted to prayer. I wanted to know God's will for my life. What did God want me to do? Was I making the correct decision in many cases? How could I hear what he was saying to me? If you are like me, sometimes you just need to hear from God, on big problems, and uncertain areas of your life. Jesus said in John 10:2-5, 11 that he that entereth in by the door is the shepherd of the sheep. The Sheep hear His voice: and He calleth his own sheep by name and leadeth them out. And a stranger will they not follow, but will flee from him: for they know not the voice of strangers. I am the good shepherd: the good shepherd giveth his life for the sheep.

Being saved opens us up to hearing God's voice. Isaiah 30:21 says that your ears hear a word behind thee saying, This is the way, walk ye in it, when ye turn to the right hand and when ye turn to the left. Yes we can hear God's voice! Thank you, Jesus for this great blessing! A simple way to hear God's voice is just go to Him in prayer taking all your burdens to him, all your worries, doubts, and needs. Ask Him a question that you need an answer on and He will answer you. Ask the question and be silent. Be silent until you hear Him.

In my own prayer life I asked if I would be successful in a business venture I was planning. The business was just a dream, just a start up. After asking I remained silent for several seconds and then I heard, Yes you will be successful in this business and long as you follow my commandments and love me with all your heart soul and mind. I said Lord is this you? Or is this my mind just wishing this would come true. He said it again and I listened. I heard this three times. Now 20 years later that business is a thriving, successful, highly respected, robust, business! Praise God. God before Him. Trust His word in Isaiah and in John that we will talk with you today and He will. Ask Him for his direction and then listen! God himself will direct your steps in life and you listen to our great and awesome God!

23

TRUST THE LORD

So many things today can make one worried. The world around us is in constant turmoil. The stock market is up and then it's down. The economy is doing well, but could fall into recession. Your job may be a good one, but technology may replace your position. Health insurance is getting so expensive, and coverages are less. There are rumors of war, forest fires, earthquakes, personal family issues, health issues, and more. So how can a person not worry, in the crazy world in which we live? Well it all begins in understanding God's Word, the Bible, is absolute truth. That you can trust God at His word. That He loves you and has a great plan for your life. Not one of worry and doubt, but one of peace and hope for a great future! In the Bible there are 365 verses that tell us not to worry, one for each day of the year!

In Matthew 6:25 Jesus tells us not to worry. "Therefore, I tell you, do not worry about your life, what you will eat or drink or about your body what you will wear." In Matthew 6:26 Jesus says God will provide what we need. "Look at the birds of the air; they do not sow or reap or store away in barns, and yet our heavenly Father feeds them. Are you not much more valuable than they?" Jesus again says not to worry – He knows we need things. In Matthew 6:31: "So do not worry, saying what shall we eat? Or what shall we drink? Or what shall we wear?" 32: For the pagans run after all these things and your Heavenly Father knows you need them.

The key verse is Matthew 6:33: "But seek first His Kingdom and His righteousness, and all these things will be given to you as well." If you will make God first place in your life over everything else, He promises that all these things shall be given us! So, if you are worried about anything today, just take it before God, lay it at His feet in prayer, and trust Him. He has promised to take care of you! Trust him by keeping your eyes, heart, and mind focused on Jesus, then everything will work out for you! Remember God's word is Truth and God promises to take care of you! Blessing for a trustful day in the Lord!

24

DON'T GIVE UP 5 MINUTES
BEFORE YOUR MIRACLE

Miracles happen every day! If you are praying for something or someone in your life, keep on praying! Keep believing! Don't give up! So many Christians give up, just before they receive the miracle that they need from our heavenly Father! In the below passages from Luke 18, Jesus provides a key to answered prayer! Be blessed as you read this wonderful understanding from our Lord and Savior!

Jesus said in Luke 18:
[1] And he spake a parable unto them to this end, that men ought always to pray, and not to faint.

[2] There was in a city a judge, which feared not God, neither regarded man:

[3] And there was a widow in that city; and she came unto him, saying, Avenge me of mine adversary.

[4] And he would not for a while: but afterward he said within himself, Though I fear not God, nor reqard man;

[5] Yet because this widow troubleth me, I will avenge her, lest by her continual coming she weary me.

[6] And the Lord said, Hear what the unjust judge saith.

[7] And shall not God avenge his own elect, which cry day and night unto him, though he bear long with them?

[8] I tell you that he will avenge them speedily. Nevertheless, when the Son of man cometh, shall he find Faith on the earth?

Jesus was teaching us to be persistent in our prayers. Keep crying out to God like the widow woman kept going before the Judge. Her persistence won her case! Persistence prayer wins as we keep believing God for answered prayer. Some of our prayers are answered so quickly and some I have been praying about for years. No matter, God's timing is always perfect, and his answers to our prayers are always perfect as well. Don't give up 5 minutes before your miracle! Your miracle is about to happen! God is about to answer your persistent faithful prayer! Keep believing God!

25

GOD CAN HEAL A BROKEN HEART

Romans 15:13: May the God of Hope fill you with all JOY and PEACE as you TRUST IN HIM, so that you may OVERFLOW with HOPE by the power of the Holy Spirit!

In this life we all encounter many trials and tribulations! The loss of a loved one, financial devastation, health issues, the loss of a job, the loss of your home, a broken relationship, divorce, a wayward child, betrayal, slander, rejection, lies about us, bad personal decisions, and even sin in our own lives, can cause us great heartache and guilt! All of this is true, but God is greater than our problems and able to heal your broken heart!

Psalms 34:18 says: The Lord is nigh unto them that are of a broken heart; and saveth such as be of a contrite spirit. This Bible verse promises that God is close to those who have a broken heart, who have lost all hope, and He will save them. Here are some helpful steps to mend a broken heart.

#1. Accept Jesus' Healing words. John 16:33: Jesus said, I have told you all this, so that you may have PEACE in ME. Here on earth you will have many trials and sorrows. But take heart, because I have overcome the World.

#2. Accept God's comfort through the Holy Spirit by talking and praying to God daily! Acts 9:31: And in the comfort of the Holy Spirit they continued to increase. Share your hurt with God and He will comfort you through His Holy Spirit!

#3. Take every Negative thought captive under the authority of Jesus Christ! 2nd Cor 10:5: Change your language to positive language by taking every thought and word captive as unto the Lord. Work on changing your bad thinking and negative talk to God's Bible promises. ETCH the positive words in the Bible on your HEART!

#4. Start praising Him in the midst of your sorrow! For all the wonderful people, blessings, answered prayers, the love of God in your life. All of the material blessings, for your health and the health of others in your family!

#5. Start doing for others, giving back in the Lord and all through His power! Receive the Healing of your heart now by focusing on him and not your problems! Practice discipline, by Reading your Bible, confessing scripture, staying in prayer, fellowship time with the Saints and doing for others.

26

SUDDENLY GOD WILL ANSWER
YOUR PRAYERS

In Acts chapter 16, Paul and Silas had been thrown in jail for preaching the Gospel. They had been seized, stripped, and beaten with rods. They didn't know what would happen to them, but they kept praying and trusting God. In the natural it looked like they could be in prison forever or, worse, put to death. But in jail they were praying and singing hymns to God when very suddenly their prayers were answered by an earthquake the Lord sent to free them.

In Acts 16:26: **Suddenly** there was such a violent earthquake that the foundations of the prison were shaken. At once all the doors flew open and everyone's chains came loose. Suddenly, their prayers were answered.

If you have been praying for a short time or a long time, just know that God hears your prayer and **suddenly**, your prayers will be answered. In God's perfect timing, in His perfect will for you, he will fulfill your prayer with His perfect answer for you. Some prayers are answered very quickly, and some answered prayers take time. Whatever God's timing is, just keep being faithful and watch the hand of God answer your prayers! You will be amazed at how God works, and how answered prayer will grow your Faith in God and become a source of great strength in your life!

27

GOD IS STILL IN THE MIRACLE SAVING BUSINESS!

What miracle do you need? Take it to God! He is still in the miracle saving business! In my own life, I have been faced with so many circumstances that were out of control and big problems that from a human standpoint were impossible, but God was always there! What seemed to be such an incredible problem in my life, was taken care of through the power of prayer! God made a way!

Remember God's word in Hebrews 13:8: Jesus Christ is the same yesterday, and today and forever. God does not change. He can still do a miracle for you! Keep praying and asking him!

John 5:14 says, "This is the confidence we have in approaching God: if we ask anything according to His Will, He hears us. And if we know that He hears us, whatever we ask we know that we have what we asked of Him."

God is listening to our prayers. We must step out in Faith. Matthew 9:29 says, "Let it be done unto according to your Faith."

God will answer your prayer in His mighty power and in His timing. God's answer may not be what you expected, but keep on trusting Him and watch the mighty hand of God work things out for you! Just like in Matthew 14 where Jesus feeds 5,000 people with only two fish and five loaves of bread. The disciples thought it was impossible to feed 5,000 people with such a little amount of food, but they didn't realize that Jesus is the God of Miracles! After Jesus blesses the food the disciples distribute the food to the 5,000 and the Bible says in Matthew 14:20: "Then all ate and were satisfied, and the disciples picked up twelve baskets of broken pieces that were left over." What a Miracle! If God can do that, He can provide a miracle for you and a blessing that will fulfill your every need. Keep taking the issue before God, trusting Him for your miracle! He will do what's best for you and your situation! He is worthy of your trust and faith in Him! Your miracle is on its way!

28

FAITH THAT PLEASES GOD

Placing our Faith fully in Jesus Christ. In Hebrews 11:6 the Bible says, "Without faith it is impossible to please Him: for he that cometh to God must believe that He is, and that He is a rewarder of them that diligently seek Him." In John 6:29, Jesus says, "This is the work of God, that ye BELIEVE in HIM whom He hath sent." Meaning that Faith that pleases God, is Faith in Jesus Christ, the Son of God whom God sent.

I have come to the conclusion that I can't trust in anything but Jesus Christ. Neither can you, if you're a believer in Christ. No one can be sure of their job, their finances, the government, the economy, even one's next breath. At times friends and family with let you down. Material things are a blessing but will not satisfy. Nor will position, power, or a career stop one from wondering, is this all there is to life? I feel so empty. Without accepting Christ as your Savior by faith, without becoming a Spirit-filled believer, without fully trusting God, our lives tend to stay in constant turmoil and without real hope. If you're a believer God wants you to have a victory-filled life with great confidence in Him. In John 10:10 Jesus says "I have come to give them life and more abundantly." God didn't want us to be a victim in life, but without totally trusting Him as the Source of our Strength, as our great provider, as our everything in life, we will miss the mark. No, we must turn our eyes upon Jesus, the source of our lives. Trust in Him for all things. Be dedicated to Him and Him alone and He will be so pleased with our Faith in Him.

My favorite FAITH story in the Bible is about a centurion's servant being healed by Jesus. It's found in Matthew chapter 8. The centurion pleads to Jesus to heal his servant and Jesus answers him saying in Matthew 8:7: I will come and heal him. Then the centurion replies, "Lord, I am not worthy that thou shouldest come under my roof: but speak the word only and my servant shall be healed. For I am a man under authority, having soldiers goeth; and to another, come and he cometh and to my servant, Do this and he doeth it. When Jesus heard this he said, Verily I have not found so great faith, no, not in Israel, God thy way and as thou hast believed, so be it done unto thee." The centurion's servant is healed that same hour. The point of this Bible promise is that Faith pleases God when you trust Him for every part of your life. Jesus Christ is life changing. He is the source of everything you will ever need. Keep pleasing God by having Faith in Him!

29

TURN TO CHRIST, HE IS
THE ANSWER

I want to talk to you today about turning your whole life over to Jesus Christ. To surrender every door, every worry, every doubt, every fear, ever burden, every relationship, every dream, everything about you to Jesus. To make Him the Lord over everything in your life.

Romans 10:9-10 says,
9 If you declare with your mouth, "Jesus is Lord," and believe in your heart that God raised Him from the dead, you will be saved. 10 For it is with your heart that you believe and are justified, and it is with your mouth that you profess your faith and are saved.

Do you remember a time when you gave your heart to the Lord Jesus Christ? Do you remember the day, the date, the moment? If not, I would like you to be sure you are born again like Jesus said in John 3:3: Verily, verily I say unto thee, Except a man be born again, he cannot see the kingdom of God.

Make sure you have accepted Him as Lord and Savior and are written in the book of Life. Meaning that you know you have eternal life through faith in Jesus Christ and in no other name.

You may attend church every week and still, no one has ever asked this question. If you died today, would you know without any doubt that you would have a place in Heaven? To be sure, just say this sinner's prayer to become saved! If you have already made that decision, please pass this on to someone else who needs the Lord.

Just repeat these words to God: Lord Jesus I know I am a sinner. I know I need a Savior! Lord, I ask you to come into my life and be the Lord over all my life. I know you were crucified for my sins, you were buried and arose from the dead on the third day! I know you are the son of God. Lord, please accept my prayer in Jesus' Holy and precious name! Amen! If you said this prayer, you are born again and are now in the kingdom of God. Be sure to get baptized and go to a Bible believing church who believes in Jesus Christ as Lord and Savior! My heart jumps for Joy every time someone makes this incredible life-changing decision to become a born-again believer in Jesus Christ! Blessings to you!

30

FAITH THAT MOVES MOUNTAINS!

What crisis are you facing? Do you have a storm in your life? Are you losing all hope? As Christians our unbelief in Christ can sometimes get in the way of God working His will through us on a daily basis. It's the Job of the Christian to believe in the one whom God sent, Jesus Christ, and to believe His WORD! John 6:29.

In Matthew 17, a man brought his son to the disciples to be healed, but the disciples could not heal him. So the man brings his son to Jesus with the same request and He heals the son. After the healing, the disciples ask Jesus why they couldn't heal the son.

In Matthew 17:20, Jesus said unto them, "Because of your unbelief: verily I say unto you, **If ye have faith as a grain of mustard seed**, ye shall say unto this mountain, Remove hence to yonder place; and it shall be removed; and nothing shall be Impossible unto you."

All Jesus is asking us is to believe in him and His WORD. Our faith, even if it's only the size of a mustard seed which is very small, is BIG ENOUGH to MOVE mountains! Just a small amount of Faith pleases God and is powerful! So no matter what you are facing today, don't believe those negative thoughts, those negative voices, those around you who keep telling you that it can't be done. Place your trust in Jesus Christ, the Savior of the World, and know that just a little FAITH on our part without doubting can move the mountains, storms, and trials from our life! Jesus will see you through!

31

ADVERSITY STRENGTHENS OUR FAITH

Setbacks and adversity are the training ground for our next promotion! Many times, setbacks are God's way of setting us up for our next Promotion in Life! You may have been treated unfairly, maybe unappreciated, passed over for a promotion you deserved, maybe you've lost your job, maybe your finances are hurting, maybe you have a broken relationship, a broken heart, or a health issue. Whatever adversity is going on in your life, just know it's not by chance. GOD sometimes allows tests, trials, and adversity to teach us, to strengthen our Faith, and to move us to the BEST Plan He has for our lives!

In Genesis, Joseph had been sold into slavery by his brothers, falsely accused of something he didn't do, and placed in prison! In the natural, the hurt must have been unbearable, but Joseph kept his FAITH in GOD. He trusted God even during those tough times and tough years of his life! Then one day the Pharaoh chose Joseph (God's man) as second in command over all of Egypt! In one day, Joseph went from working in the Prison to living in the Palace!

The Bible says in Genesis 40:39-41:

39 So Pharaoh said to Joseph, "Since God has informed you of all this, there is no one so discerning and wise as you are."
40 "You shall be over my house, and according to your command all my people shall do homage; only in the throne I will be greater than you."
41 Pharaoh said to Joseph, "See, I have set you over all the land of Egypt."

Don't let adversity slow you down! Keep your Faith in Jesus Christ! Keep believing! Keep trusting God! Your current adversity maybe really tough, but I believe God is working out His Will and purpose for your life for His Glory! Give your current trial over to God! You can trust that His perfect will for your life is the best plan! I believe your best days are ahead of you! God is planning something Great for your life! I am praying for your success! Just like Joseph, you will go from the prison to your new promotion into the palace! Keep trusting the Lord for your deliverance!

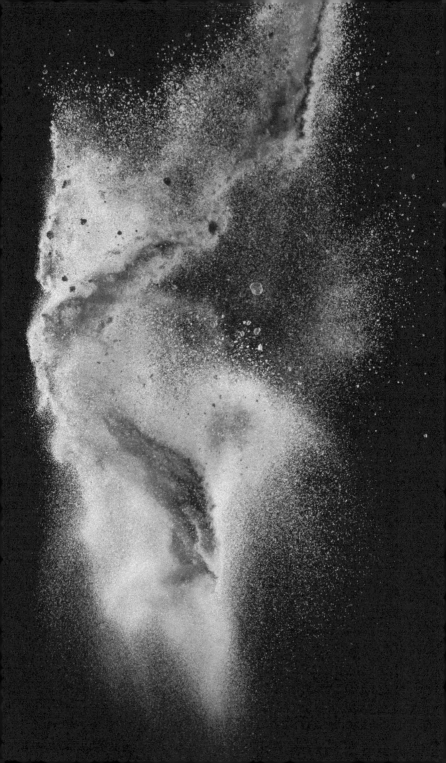

32

EVERY MORNING, START WITH GOD FIRST!

Mornings can sometimes be a struggle for anyone, especially if one is focused on the problems of the week like loneliness, bad weather, health issues, trials we are facing, or overall negative thoughts filling our minds. Focusing on those fearful, down, depressing, thoughts can ruin anyone's day. Be sure to take every thought captive unto Christ in prayer each day. So many of my friends ask me how do you stay so POSITIVE? And I tell them that I start each morning BY talking with God.

Every morning when I first wake up, lying in bed, I say, Good morning, God. I start out by thanking Him for the day, praising His Holy name, acknowledging how awesome He is, and asking Him to lead me, guide me, to take away any bad thoughts, depressing thoughts, or stinking thinking, that I might have rolling around in my head. I ask Him to help me to have a positive attitude and enjoy every day. I lay down all of my burdens

before Jesus Christ and my FAITH and HOPE skyrocket upward. I go from being down and sad, to up and excited about my day. I pray in bed and after a wonderful time in prayer with the Lord, my feet hit the floor with a new hope, a new optimism, and a new excitement, and with a thankful heart!

This is so easy to do. Start out each day with the Lord in Prayer! Then get your Bible out and look up one of your favorite Bible promises that inspires you for that day. When I pick out a Bible verse, I focus on it for the rest of the day and, believe me, it inspires me and makes my day go well! I challenge you to make this change and talk with God every morning and I promise each day will be a blessing to you!

Like Matthew 6:34: Do not be anxious about tomorrow, for tomorrow, for tomorrow will be anxious for itself. Sufficient for the day is its own trouble.

33

COMMIT YOUR PLANS TO GOD
FOR SUCCESS!

Proverbs 16:33 says Commit your plans before THE LORD and HE will make them a success!

In anything I attempt in life, I first bring my plan to God and I surrender it to His leadership. My company A3 Marketing has been highly successful over 20 years and I give all the credit to God. When He controls your company and your financial destiny, you can be sure of your success! His Bible promises are true. One great example of this is a popular fast food restaurant chain.. Their leadership has surrendered every location and plan they have to God. They are only open 6 days a week so that employees can go to church on Sundays, while all their competition is open 7 days a week and yet they are one of the most successful fast food chains in the world! When God gives you a promise, He keeps his promise to His children!

Don't go it alone. With any big plan in your life, like moving, changing jobs, making a big purchase, opening a new business, marrying someone, or investing in something, be sure to take your plan before God. Make God your partner and ask Him to be your CEO/CFO and watch your plans succeed!

Remember Proverbs 16:33: Commit your plans before the Lord and He WILL MAKE THEM A SUCCESS!

34

GOD'S DIVINE CALL ON
YOUR LIFE!

Acts 9

God has a Divine call on your life! He is the infinite, all powerful and eternal God! He has a call and a will for everyone's life, but sadly, so many Christians never mature into the fulfilled, confident, secure, content, and joyful Christian God wants them to become.

Then there are those in the World that have not been born again. They haven't made a commitment for Christ! They are lost without God, without His guidance, without His presence! Without the security of a Heavenly home. They need the Savior, but Sin and the World have them caught up in a lifestyle dictated by the world's standard of success. Tossed and turned by every superstition, false religion, false teaching like karma, voodoo, crystals, Satan Worship, the occult, black magic, witchcraft, Scientology, aliens, political religion, and more. They are still searching and asking what is my purpose? They are still wondering why am I here? Many people compare their lives against others on the basis of what they have or don't have. Feeling unfulfilled because they are not married, not wealthy, not famous, not driving the right car,

no children, not out of debt, and on and on.

God's divine call or plan for every person in the world is to have a personal relationship with Jesus Christ to forgive their sins, to secure a place in heaven for them, and to have the abundant life that Jesus promised in John 10:10: "I am come that they might have life, and that they might have it more abundantly." Philippians 2:13: "For it is God which worketh in you both to will and to do of his good pleasure." Romans 12:1: "I beseech you therefore, brethren, by the mercies of God, that ye present your bodies a living sacrifice, holy, acceptable unto God, which is your reasonable service. And be not conformed to this world: but be ye transformed by the renewing of your mind, that ye may prove what is that good, and acceptable, and perfect, will of God."

Surrender your life to Jesus Christ! He will help you to mature into the fulfilled, confident, secure, content, and joyful Christian you were made to become. God's divine call for your life is God's best plan for you!

35

FIGHT EVERY BATTLE ON YOUR KNEES FOR VICTORY!

When faced with a real battle such as a financial difficulty, a loss of job, a health issue, a death in the family, or something else, no matter what difficulty you are going through, here are some steps to victory! In 2nd Chronicles Chapter 20, Jehoshaphat, King of Judah, is being attacked by a great army that is sure to destroy his kingdom and kill his people. The armies coming against him were around 180,000 men versus his army of just 30,000 men. An alarmed King Jehoshaphat takes this problem before God in prayer. God tells the king through a prophet named Jahaziel that the battle is not his and that God will fight the battle for him. Drastic times require drastic measures so King Jehoshaphat tells all of his family and the people in his kingdom to come before the Lord in prayer and fasting with him. When faced with a big battle we must be diligent, we must be persistent, we must go before the living God and ask for His help in our time of need! It worked for King Jehoshaphat and it will work for you! You can win this battle with God!

Please read 2 Chronicles Chapter 20:1-30 to gain a full understanding of this wonderful teaching and the steps below.

1. Faced with a Battle – Go to God on your knees about the problem first. Cry out to God for help!

2. Praise God for His sovereignty, His Power, and His Might.

3. Stand on the WORD of GOD – Trust His Word! Isaiah 54:17: Remember no weapon formed against you shall prosper! God is Great! Take all your battles to God for Victory!

4. Listen to God for the Battle is not yours!

5. Be Humble, Have a contrite Heart toward God!

6. Have Faith – Trust God to give you the Victory!

36

GOD'S PROMISES ARE TRUE!

I am so thankful that I truly know with all my heart that every word of the Bible is Truth! God has clearly shown me in my personal and business life that you can know without a doubt that every Bible promise is true.

Remember what 2nd Corinthians 1:20 says; For ALL the PROMISES of God in Him are YES, and in Him Amen, to the glory of God through us.

The above scripture absolutely tells us in God's word that all of His promises are true!

When the world, or voices in your head, or others in your life say to you that things won't work out, that you're not worthy, that you will never achieve your dreams, don't believe these false voices. Go to God's Word and pull out those Bible promises that address what you are going through. God is with you and He will see you through!

Read Luke 18:27 over and over today! Replace any doubt in your head, with God's Word below!

Jesus replied, "What is impossible with man is possible with God." A very powerful scripture, from an awesome and all-powerful GOD! He is with you today! Trust His Word!

37

THE ANOINTING OF GOD ON YOUR LIFE

Being anointed is a very special blessing from God through His Holy Spirit. In the New Testament, all believers receive the Holy Spirit when they accept Jesus Christ as Lord and Savior.

The Bible says in Ephesians 1:13: In whom ye also trusted, after that ye heard the word of truth, the gospel of your salvation: in whom also after that ye believed, ye were sealed with that Holy Spirit of promise. As soon as someone gives their heart to Jesus Christ, they receive the Holy Spirit.

Jesus said in John 14-15: If you love me, keep my commandments.
[16] And I will pray the Father, and he shall give you another comforter, that he may abide with you forever;
[17] Even the Spirit of truth; whom the world cannot receive, because it seeth him not, neither knoweth him: but ye know him; for he dwelleth with you and shall be in you.

As a Christian the Holy Spirit lives inside of you. Leading you, guiding you, blessing you, teaching you His truth, His knowledge, His wisdom, His will for your life and much more! It's God way of communicating with us. Since Jesus Christ is no longer in the flesh on earth and now resides in Heaven, He promised to not leave us alone. He said He would send us the Holy Spirit and He did!

In John 4:24 God is a Spirit: and they that worship him must worship him in Spirit and in truth.

So communicate with God by walking in the Spirit, praying in the Spirit and you will know what His will is for your life! Get before Him in prayer, talking with Him as you go through your day. Listen for His voice in all decisions. Follow the Holy Spirit! He will direct your steps!

38

OVERCOMING ANXIETY

Overcoming anxiety is one of the great benefits of having a personal relationship with Jesus Christ. Are you a person that worries all the time? Do you have anxiety attacks? Are you fearful and can't seem to trust God to meet all your needs? Are you always thinking negative down thoughts? Do you live with worry and fear about your future? If so, I can truly help you overcome anxiety if you will follow the below steps.

1. Find a place alone to prayer to God each day. Prayer is the key to connecting to God and He will fill you with His Holy Spirit! His presence brings Peace and rids your mind and heart of worry and doubt! Just ask Him to take away all fear and he will each day in prayer.

2. Pray three times a day to God if you are experiencing anxiety. Don't get up off your knees until fear is replaced with Joy and Trust! Dedication is the key to go from Fear to great Faith.

3. Read all the positive verses in the Bible. Each one will strengthen your Faith by the renewing of your mind. Romans 12:1: Be dedicated to this every day. Read Bible promises like Philippians 4:13: I can do all things through Christ who strengthens me!

4. Be sure to eat healthy foods. Be sure to get at least 20 minutes of exercise 5 days a week. Be sure to get enough sleep; doctors suggest 8 hours or more.

5. Protect your mind from negative thoughts. When you think a negative fearful thought, stop it at the imaginary gate of your mind, and don't accept it. Replace all negative thoughts with positive thoughts in the Bible. That means read your Bible every day! Also protect your mind by not filling it with bad things like scary movies, negative people, negative news reports, unwholesome jokes, and more. The Bible in Philippians says for all of us to think on good things.

6. Get a prayer partner to pray with. I suggest someone that is powerful in the Lord and a very Godly person. Remember that there is power in prayer and especially when two or more are gathered together for prayer. Matthew 18:20 says "For where two or three are gathered together in my name, there am I in the midst of them."

39

P E A C E
IN
GOD

Place all your worries and doubts into the Master's Hand, Jesus Christ! Peace cannot be purchased! If you have no peace in your life go before GOD and release every burden to Him. Surrender everything to Him and Peace will be yours! Remember Jesus Christ is called the PRINCE OF PEACE.

In Isaiah 9:6: "For unto us a child is born, unto us a son is given: and the government shall be upon his shoulder: and his name shall be called Wonderful, Counsellor, The mighty God, The everlasting Father, **The Prince of Peace.**"

Jesus said in John 14:27: "Peace I leave with you; my peace I give unto you. I do not give to you as the world gives. Do not let your hearts be troubled and do not be afraid."

So tonight, don't be afraid of anything! Rest easy on your pillow knowing that your heavenly Father is watching over you! Accept the peace of God by turning all your burdens over to Him! Peace be with you!

40

HE HAS RISEN – REJOICE THAT CHRIST HAS RISEN!

John 20:1, and John 20:11-16

¹Now on the first day of the week Mary Magdalene went to the tomb early, while it was still dark, and saw that the stone had been taken away from the tomb. ¹¹But Mary stood outside by the tomb weeping and as she wept she stooped down and looked into the tomb. ¹²And she saw two angels in white sitting, one at the head and the other at the feet, where the body of Jesus had lain. ¹³Then they said to her, Woman why are you weeping? She said because they have taken away my Lord, and I do not know where they have laid Him. ¹⁴Now when she had said this, she turned around and saw Jesus standing there and did not know that it was Jesus. ¹⁵Jesus said to her Woman why are you weeping? Whom are you seeking? She supposing Him to be the gardener, said to Him, Sir, if you have carried Him away, tell me where you have laid Him, and I will take Him away. ¹⁶Jesus said to her, Mary! She turned and said to Him Rabboni! Which is to say teacher. Mary's eyes were opened and recognized Jesus! He had risen! He was alive! Just like he foretold before going to the Cross for the forgiveness of sins for all of mankind.

Becoming a Christian is the greatest thing that ever happened to my life. I remember the day so well, when I heard the knocking of the Holy Spirit of God on my heart saying, you need me, I am your Lord and Savior. And so that day, I got up out of my seat in church at the hearing of the Gospel and gave my heart to Jesus Christ at the altar. I was 10 years old. What a great Savior we have! I am so thankful to be written in the Book of Life that gives me a guarantee of a place in heaven and that He has been my Savior for over 50 years! Do you know for sure that if you died today that you would go to heaven? If you do, that's great, but if you have never made the decision to follow Jesus Christ as your personal Savior and Lord, you should make that decision today.

In John 3:16 Jesus said that God so loved the World that He gave His only begotten Son, that whosoever believeth in Him would not perish but have everlasting life.

If you are a Christian, rejoice that He has Risen from the dead proving that He is God and that He is our Savior! Share your experience with others, so that they may become born again! Rejoice! We serve the living God!

41

MONEY GOD'S WAY!

I believe the whole Bible to be true! If you are like me you believe in the Virgin birth of Jesus, you believe in the miracles of Jesus, you believe that Jesus Christ is the Savior of the World, and was crucified, buried, and raised from the dead on the third day. You believe He died on the cross for the forgiveness of sins so that we who are saved can have an eternal home in Heaven.

If you believe all these things and more than consider the blessing of Money God's way! God wants a total surrender of every subject in your life, including your money. When we surrender our financial future with God as our partner, He blesses it beyond what we could even ask or think!

In Malachi 3:10 the Bible says: Bring the whole tithe into the storehouse, that there may be food in my house. Test me in this, says the Lord Almighty and see if I will not throw open the floodgates of heaven and pour out so much blessing that there will not be room enough to store it.

[11] I will prevent pests from devouring your crops, and the vines in your fields will not drop their fruit before it is ripe, says the Lord Almighty.
[12] Then all the nations will call you blessed for yours will be a delightful land, says the Lord Almighty.

All of my Christian friends who tithe are always blessed more than those that do not tithe. Why? Because God wants total obedience in all areas of our life. If you are living paycheck to paycheck, then test God in this area of your life and see that by giving God the first 10% of all you make, that He will open the floodgates of Heaven and pour out so much blessing you will not have room to contain it. Trust God! All of God's promises in the Bible are true even about money!

42

GOD'S CREATION AND YOU!

Genesis 1:1: In the beginning GOD created the heaven and the earth. And the earth was without form, and void; and darkness was upon the face of the deep. And the Spirit of GOD moved upon the face of the waters. And God said let there be light: and there was light.

God created everything and we are His creation as well. He loves you so much and created a beautiful, wonderful place called Earth for you to live. Everything in nature exalts the Lord's magnificent power to create such a beautiful universe.

Psalms 19:1 says: The Heavens declare the glory of God.

Nature was created for us to enjoy. So many times, in my own life taking a trip to the mountains in Gatlinburg, about 3 hours from our Nashville home, rejuvenates my soul, my strength, and refocuses my life on what a great God we serve. My faith is strengthened! I feel the same way at the ocean or walking through the forest. God is to be praised and worshipped for His greatness and the wonderful gifts of the Earth He created for us. The main point I want to make to you today is for more peace and enjoyment in your life, get out into nature and away from all phones, TVs, tablets, and your responsibilities. Get away like Jesus always did by getting into nature and directing your thoughts, prayers, and worship unto God for His wonderful creation and all he has done for you. Remember we are all part of His great creation and it's in nature that we can find a closer walk with God by getting alone with Him. Take at least 4 trips a year away from work even if they are weekend trips to restore and revitalize your soul!

Stay Positive AND Good THinGS Will HaPPen

43

STAY POSITIVE: THINK ON GOOD THINGS!

Are you a positive person? When you think or say things about your future, are they hopeful words? Do you speak encouraging words to yourself and to others? The Bible specifically says that we should think and say good things. Be a positive force in the world. Speak life into yourself, your family, and to others.

Philippians 4:8 says:
⁸ Finally, brethren, whatsoever things are true, whatsoever things are honest, whatsoever things are just, whatsoever things are pure, whatsoever things are lovely, whatsoever things are of good report; if there be any virtue, and if there be any praise, think on these things.

You see, God wants us to renew our minds with His Word. All negative thoughts should be placed captive unto God.

God wants you to be hopeful each day, because He has a great hope and future for your tomorrow.

The Bible says in 2 Corinthians 10:5:
⁵ Casting down imaginations, and every high thing that exalteth itself against the knowledge of God, and bringing into captivity every thought to the obedience of Christ

All thoughts, all words should come under God's authority and if you do, your life will become a positive productive force of encouragement and hope for yourself and others! Don't let any thoughts of doubt, fear, hate, negativity fill your mind. No, fill your mind with all the great words in the Bible and walk in Faith and not doubt. Have a great positive day!

44

GOD'S FAVOR AND BLESSINGS!

To get the full favor of God is to walk so close to Him that your walk is blameless. No one is perfect, but what I am talking about is knowing that you are sinning and you continue to go against God and His word about sin in your life. If you or someone you know is living this way, then you can tell that their lives are messed up and they are having many troubles. Not all troubles are brought upon us for sinning, but many troubles are. In this life we will experience suffering, but I just don't want to bring trouble unto myself for disobeying God and His Word.

The Bible says in Psalms 84:11:
[11] For the Lord God is a sun and shield: the Lord will give grace and glory: no good thing will be withhold from them that walk uprightly.

So God is a God of love and since He loves us so, He will not put up with sin in our lives. If we repent and turn away from our Sin, He will forgive us and bring His FAVOR upon us for following His Word. If we continue in our sin, for instance, lying about your taxes, having an affair, drinking too much, using bad language on a continual basis, slandering others, or even not coming to church, these are just a few sins that can keep us from God's best. God wants us to obey Him, and if we do, we will have His utmost favor and blessing!

To restore yourself back into a right relationship with God, go before him and confess your sin. He will forgive you right away and restore all things to you!

The Bible says in 1 John 1:9:
[9] If we confess our sins, he is faithful and just to forgive us our sins, and to cleanse us from all unrighteousness.

45

GOD'S LOVE FOR THE BELIEVER!

Throughout my life whenever I have felt down, defeated, or depressed about my circumstances or who I am, I turned to God. Many things in life are unfair and unjust. Most people never get the appreciation they deserve in life by mere people.

We should never depend on a person or the world in general for our self-worth. When you go to God, He tells you how wonderfully made you are. He lets you know what a great future and a hope He has for you. He died on the Cross so that ours sins are forgiven, and so that we would have an eternal home in heaven with Him one day. **Remember, our trust should be in God and not in man, or money, or career.**

For the Bible says; What is impossible with man is possible with God. So if you are feeling down or depressed over your situation today, remember to trust what God says and not others! God will never let you down. This isn't the end of your story, God has great plans for you! Here are some scriptures that can help you see how valuable and loved you are by God.

Psalms 139:14:
[14] I will praise thee; for I am fearfully and wonderfully made: marvellous are thy works; and that my soul knoweth right well.

Jeremiah 29:11:
[11] For I know the thoughts that I think toward you, saith the Lord, thoughts of peace, and not of evil, to give you an expected end.

46

BREAK FREE FROM THE BONDAGE OF THE PAST BY FORGIVING OTHERS

Break FREE from the bondage of the past by Forgiving others who have hurt you. FREE yourself from all bitterness, resentment, sadness, and the hate that it produces. Some people have been mad at each other for so long, that they can't really remember what they are upset over. Others have been abused as a child, falsely accused for something they didn't do, fired from a job for no reason, had a hurtful divorce, or had a family member write them off and not talk with them for years. Many times, from a human standpoint, forgiveness doesn't seem possible or make sense.

But God is a God of restoration. He wants us FREE from the bondage of unforgiveness. Go to the Lord and ask Him to help you forgive the person that sinned against you. Jesus said in Matthew 18:22 that we were to forgive others 7 x 70. Not once, not twice, but 7 x 70 times. Not forgiving others just keeps us in a constant turmoil that can hold us back from God's best for our lives! God can heal your broken heart. He can make a new beginning! Just start the healing process by being obedient to God's Word. Forgive others and be forgiven!

I know that many terrible things have happened, but God doesn't want your life infected and frozen in the past. He wants you healed of your past. He wants you to trust Him instead of your emotions. When God sent His only Son to die on the cross, to be buried and raised from the dead on the third day, He made a way through the Holy Spirit and the Word of God to overcome all of these problems. Our job is to fully surrender to His will and to His Glory each day! God loves you and wants you to break FREE from all past sorrows! Walk away from past hurts today and into the Joy of the Lord!!! Break FREE today! Blessings to you all! Love you in the Lord!

47

YOUR HOPE AND STRENGTH COMES FROM THE LORD

Do not lose HOPE! Your HOPE and STRENGTH comes from the LORD! God is saying, those who HOPE in ME WILL RENEW their STRENGTH and WILL SOAR like EAGLES!

Sometimes during difficult times in our life, we can lose our strength, can become almost defeated in the natural. We grow tired and weary over the same battles day after day wondering if it will ever end. Worry, doubt, and loss of strength can be the result a prolonged illness, divorce, lawsuit, financial crisis, and more. Even though we are under attack,

God promises that is we place our HOPE in the one and True Living God, that He will renew our strength. As we trust and wait on Him, He will deliver us and we will regain a new strength through Him! Our doubts will turn to trust! Our fears will turn to Faith, our sadness will turn to joy! Prayer is supernatural and we shouldn't take our time with God lightly. Have a problem in your life today? Then Cry out to Him in your time of destress and I promise He will come to your aid and rescue you.

The Bible says in Psalms 50:15: And call upon me in the day of trouble: I will deliver thee, and thou shalt glorify me.

Regain your strength by going before God in prayer! He will help you! Do not FEAR! Take COURAGE IN THE LORD! FLY LIKE AN EAGLE!

Isaiah 40:31 King James Version: [31] But they that wait upon the Lord shall renew their strength; they shall mount up with wings as eagles; they shall run, and not be weary; and they shall walk, and not faint.

48

GOD IS YOUR SOURCE!

Do not worry! Don't let bad voices in your head keep you down!

Praise God! For **He is your source!**

He will supply your every need! God is opening new doors that only He could open! New opportunities! New breakthroughs! New resources just for you! Get excited about this new day! Make great plans with the Lord! He has an unlimited supply and He is working all things out for you!! Keep trusting! Nothing in the world can stop you if God is your Father, Savior!

The Bible says: But seek first the Kingdom of God, and His righteousness; and all these things shall be added unto you.

Matthew 6:33:
Today Seek God's kingdom first. Make God first in all you do. Make Him your first love. Place Him in charge of everything you do! All your dreams, every door of your life! Your finances, your business, your family, your heart, your mind, your soul, and everything you need will be added unto you!

Also keep realizing that He is your Source and He will supply your need!

Philippians 4:19:
But my God shall supply all your need according to His riches in glory by Christ Jesus.

49

JOY AT CHRISTMAS!

Keeping Christ, the Treasure, in your hearts at Christmas! God wants us to celebrate His Son every day, but especially at Christmas. Is your heart hurting over a prayer not answered? Do you have a loved one who doesn't follow Christ? Are you experiencing health issues? Do you have a financial crisis? Have you lost a loved one and miss them during this time of year? Is someone you know sick and you are worried about them? By keeping the TREASURE of CHRIST in our hearts at Christmas we can still experience true JOY in our HEARTS and MINDS during this season. Joy comes from the Lord and He wants every Christian to focus on Him to obtain His Joy at Christmas, the Joy of the birth of Jesus Christ and all He has done for us.

When Jesus had been born in Bethlehem, Matthew 2 the Bible says that wise men traveled many miles to see the child. To worship him! When they saw the star over the manger they were overjoyed! Because the Savior of all of mankind was born! When the wise men saw the star over the manger, they rejoiced with exceeding GREAT JOY and then they worshipped Him.
10 When they saw the star, they rejoiced with exceeding great joy.

11 And when they were come into the house, they saw the young child with Mary his mother, and fell down, and worshipped him: and when they had opened their treasures, they presented unto him gifts; gold, and frankincense, and myrrh.

Although the wise men were over great kingdoms with many material things, they focused on the JOY of finding the Messiah, the Savior of the world. Traveling hundreds of miles for almost a year they worshiped the newborn baby, God's only Son. What are your eyes focused on at Christmas this year? Keep Jesus Christ first in your life! Keep focused on Him. Keep worshiping Him. Keep your eyes on the true Christmas Story in Matthew 2 and Joy at Christmas will be yours!

50

PEACE   AT   CHRISTMAS,   INSTEAD   OF   GRIEF

I was 11 years old when my grandfather, my best friend, had a brain aneurysm and was in a coma for many days. I prayed in the chapel at the hospital in Charlotte, North Carolina where he was and asked God to heal him. Even at this early age, I had great faith in the Lord and knew if it was God's plan, my grandfather would come back to health again. Days after my constant prayer my grandfather passed away and this was the first real death experience I had ever had. Many tears were shed at Christmas that year without Him. As a family we decided to think about all the great memories and time God had given us with such a great man. Our sadness and our grief changed to peace, as we focused on Jesus Christ and how we knew in our faith that we would see our grandfather again because of what Jesus had done on the cross and how God had raised him from the dead!

So I come from a place where I have experienced peace even in the loss of a loved one at Christmas. What about you? If you are feeling **down** look up to Jesus Christ for His peace at Christmas. There is no substitute, and He is the only way to peace through such a loss.

In Isaiah 26:3, the Bible says "Thou wilt keep him in perfect peace, whose MIND is STAYED on thee: because he trusteth in thee."

Meaning that when faced with a terrible situation, a great loss, don't focus on your loss, focus on the Lord and Peace will be yours. Praise God in your prayers and be filled with the Joy of His Presence!

This week, play Christian music, read all the passages about God's peace in the Bible and pray each day for peace. You will find great peace by staying focused on God every day!

51

TAKE COURAGE IN THE LORD!

Do not lose HOPE! Your HOPE and STRENGTH comes from the LORD! God is saying, those who HOPE in ME, WILL RENEW their STRENGTH and WILL SOAR like EAGLES!

You may be tired of the fight. You may feel like giving up. You may think about running away from your situation, but don't. Gain great strength from the Lord by going before Him in prayer and asking for renewal, for great strength, and He will help you! Do not FEAR! Take COURAGE IN THE LORD and He will help you regain your strength and soar LIKE AN EAGLE!

In Isaiah 40:31, the Bible says: But those who hope in the LORD will renew their strength. They will soar on wings like eagles; they will run and not grow weary, they will walk and not be faint.

No matter what you are facing, God has promised, that if you put your Hope in Him, you will regain your strength, soar like an eagle, your will run and not grow weary, you will walk and not be faint! Take courage; your hope is in the Lord! He will help you!

52

PRAISE, PRESENCE, AND THE
PURPOSE OF GOD IN YOUR LIFE!

Get your battery in the LORD recharged for life! By PRAISING HIM, BY STAYING IN HIS PRESENCE, AND KNOWING THE PURPOSE OF GOD for your life!   Praising God, worshipping our Lord and knowing His Will ignites His Presence, His Power and Purpose in our lives! Nothing is more exciting then walking with God! If you feel like you have missed the mark, don't worry, you're still living and have an opportunity to live for Christ!! Walk with Him and in His presence and perfect will for your life! He wants a close relationship with all of us!

FOUR SIMPLE THINGS YOU CAN DO EACH DAY FOR A CLOSER WALK WITH CHRIST!

#1. BE TOTALLY DEDICATED TO LIVING FOR THE LORD EACH DAY! The Bible says in Acts 2:47 NEW Believers praised the Lord and committed themselves to living for Christ (God's purpose and will for their lives) and God added to their number daily.

#2. PRAISE BRINGS THE PRESENCE OF GOD: WORSHIP GOD EACH DAY! Psalms 16:11: You make known to me the PATH of LIFE; in your presence there is fullness of JOY; at your right hand are pleasures forevermore.

#3. WALK IN HIS PRESENCE THROUGH HIS HOLY SPIRIT! John 14:15-16: He bridges the gap between Heaven and earth through the Holy Spirit.

#4. UNDERSTAND HIS PURPOSE FOR YOUR LIFE! Philippians 2:13: For it is God who works in you, to will, and to act on behalf of His Good purpose.

THIS WEEK SURRENDER EVERYTHING TO JESUS CHRIST, YOUR FAMILY, YOUR BUSINESS, YOUR CAREER, YOUR FUTURE, YOUR FINANCES, YOUR RELATIONSHIPS, YOUR HEART! SURRENDER EVERYTHING KNOWING THAT GOD HIMSELF IS WORKING IN YOU, THROUGH YOU, TO DO HIS WILL AND ACT ON BEHALF OF HIS GOOD PURPOSE. JUST BE PLEASING TO GOD AND FOLLOW HIS WORD! GOD CAN BE TRUSTED WITH EVERY PART OF YOUR LIFE! LIVE FOR HIM!

BE INSPIRED BY READING THE WORD

To be INSPIRED EVERY DAY OF YOUR LIFE, fill your mind with the WORD of God! READ it every day! It is the absolute INSPIRATION of GOD to mankind! This love letter from God to you will change your life forever! It will renew your mind each day! Your Faith in God will grow! You will go from doubt to confidence, from fear to Faith, from impossible to possible! The Bible is so powerful it will change the way you live, the way you talk, the way you think, and make you more Christ-like as you read its words! In its pages are life eternal through Jesus Christ the Son of GOD, wisdom, Joy, peace, patience, forgiveness, strength, and more.

THE BIBLE SAYS:
2 Timothy 3: 16-17:
[16] All scripture is given by inspiration of God, and is profitable for doctrine, for reproof, for correction, for instruction in righteousness
[17] That the man of God may be perfect, thoroughly furnished unto all good works.

Jeremiah 33:3: Call unto me, and I will answer thee, and show you great and mighty things, which thou knowst not. The Bible is clear that God wants us to read His Word and He will inspire us every day and show us great and mighty things we do not know. Read the WORD and be inspired!!!

WALKING IN THE LOVE OF THE HOLY SPIRIT!

In Matthew 22:39 Jesus said that we are to love our neighbors as ourselves. "Thou shalt love thy neighbor as thyself." Today with such busy lifestyles, we could all do better to help out our neighbors. Do you ever take something you baked or fixed for dinner to a neighbor? Do you ever invite your neighbors to visit your church for a special gathering or event? Do you ever offer to pick up their mail or cut their grass when they are on vacation? Do you ever help feed the homeless or check on a widow? Do you ever wave or give your neighbor a smile, when they drive by or walk by your home?

These are just a few examples of things you can do to share God's love with others. From a human standpoint, sometimes you may not feel like you have enough love for some of your neighbors, but as your relationship gets closer to our Lord each day, He will direct you and give you the extra love you need, to get beyond human love and share His love with others.

When we as Christians realize all that God has done for us, and all the love He has bestowed on us, to forgive us, to give us eternal life yet while we were still sinners, it's easy to love ours neighbors as ourselves.

Romans 5:8 says:
[8] But God commandeth his love toward us, in that, while we were yet sinners, Christ died for us.
Matthew 22:39 is a great commandment that Jesus gives every believer. Following Jesus Christ through the Holy Spirit, we as believers are empowered to love others as Christ loved us. We have been given His grace and we need to share what God has done for us with others.

So today bless someone you know with His word, showing compassion, love for others, forgiveness, generosity, and more with a servant leadership attitude to follow the command of God to love your neighbor as yourself. What a great witness it is to show love to our neighbors!

My Story

- FROM FEAR TO FAITH -

In 1993 my father passed away unexpectedly from a heart attack. I loved him so very much and miss him every day! He was my boss as President of Bob Williams Automotive. He was a great leader, husband, father, grandfather, brother, and businessman. He was only 61 years old and had never been sick. It was such a shock to our family. At the time, I was 33 years old and running our family's dealership in Nashville, Bob Williams Lincoln Mercury. My brothers Doug and Greg ran Bob Williams Ford Lincoln Mercury with my brother in-law Randy Nash. My Mother and my sister, Debbie Nash, helped us as well at both stores.

I was a dedicated Christian, deacon, and Sunday school teacher, but for the first time **Fear** took over my life. I was so upset with my father's passing and to make matters worse my brother, my best friend, was sick during this time as well. Fear was running my life. Fear is False Evidence Appearing Real and I was believing this false evidence. I call this type of worry and doubt, the "What if's. What if I failed? What if I couldn't run our family business? If I couldn't do the job, we would lose everything. We needed to continue to be profitable for over 165 employees that worked for us and for thousands of faithful customers, but what if I couldn't do it without Dad. I was having panic attacks, anxiety, and could hardly sleep at night. I was worrying all the time. I had no peace. I had to be rushed to the ER for these attacks and they were getting worse and worse. I was so fearful.

God, I need your help was my prayer. In 1994 I was totally transformed from **FEAR** to **FAITH**, when crying out to God in my prayer closet alone. I was crying out for peace in my life, trust, and hope for the future, and that's when it happened, *The Holy Spirit showered me with His presence, His power, His peace, and His strength.* My tears were tears of Joy that night because, I went from Fear to **Faith!**

God had changed my life forever with a visit from Him in my prayer closet. Praise God! After my prayer time was over, I went and told my wife Donna what had happened. I explained to her that I was changed. I was no longer fearful! God has taken the spirit of fear out of my life. I have His peace! She believed me and we rejoiced thanking God! Through continued Bible study and prayer with my brother in-law Southern Baptist Minister, Mike Escue, and my incredible Bob Williams Team, God gave us 7 unbelievable years of profit, success, national awards, and strength through this trial in my life. From this incredible God experience, I have a burning desire to encourage others to grow in their Christian Faith or to make a decision to follow Jesus Christ as their personal Savior. I thank God for what He has done in my life, so with a grateful heart, I want to share it with the world. This transformation has been a long and exciting surrender of my life to Him. I was ordained as a Minister by FBC Hendersonville, TN to bring the good news of Jesus Christ and my *Encouraging Moments* to the Marketplace and beyond. I want to thank Minister Richard Gaia, Dr. Bruce Chesser, and Executive Pastor Bruce Raley for making my ordination possible at FBC. I am forever humbled and grateful for these great men of God.

After 25 years our family decided to sell our dealerships. God gave me A3 Marketing our advertising company which I opened in June of 2000. Dedicating A3 Marketing to the Lord and starting from just a dream, God has positioned us in Nashville as one of the premier advertising companies to help grow some of the most prestigious companies and strengthen their brands. We are dedicated to encouraging others through A3 Marketing, and now through our new Spirit of a Champion Inc., God's 501(C)3 ministry that He has entrusted us with to share His love in the marketplace and around the world. We produced our first ENCOURAGING MOMENT WITH BOBBY WILLIAMS several years ago. I want to thank Producer Jeff Hockman, Pastor Steve Galiher, Producer Mike Green, and the blessings of my wife, Donna. God's provincial hand moved to place these on the TCT Network and now this year on NRBTV. Encouraging Moments are NOW SEEN IN OVER 100 MILLION HOMES ACROSS AMERICA! I am so thankful to the Lord for using them for His Glory! My Hope for ENCOURAGING MOMENTS with Bobby Williams is that you will find Daily Christian inspiration and encouragement for your LIFE! John 10:10. (NKJV) Jesus said, I have come that they may have life, and that they may have it more abundantly! This is my prayer for you! I love you in the Lord!

You can find Encouraging Moments with Bobby Williams across the TCT and NRBTV television networks, Youtube, Roku, Instagram, or Facebook.com/spiritofachampion. He also reaches thousands with his weekly 20-minute audio Podcast which can be found on iTunes, Spotify, and iHeartradio.